☆☆☆☆☆☆☆☆☆☆☆☆☆☆☆☆☆☆☆☆☆☆☆☆☆☆☆☆☆☆☆☆☆☆

American
MILITARY
UNIFORMS

1639-1968

A COLORING BOOK
BY PETER F. COPELAND

★★★★★★★★★★★★★★★★★★★★★★★★★★★★★★★★★★

DOVER PUBLICATIONS, INC.
New York

To Ingrid Lorrain Jonsson

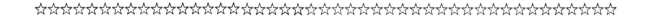

INTRODUCTION

Modern military uniforms can be traced back to ancient times. Originally one of the reasons for clothing soldiers in uniforms was to help distinguish friend from foe in the heat of battle. In addition to insuring that soldiers were appropriately dressed and equipped for action, uniforms were also thought to contribute to esprit de corps. Elegant uniform dress was also effective as an inducement for recruiting purposes.

Military uniforms have existed in the United States since colonial times. Troops were raised in the American colonies in the early seventeenth century. Some attempt was made to establish a form of uniform dress, or symbol of recognition, for the troops to wear, even though this was before the time when all soldiers wore uniforms. Early in the eighteenth century companies of soldiers were raised in various colonies, some in uniform but most without. Many of these troops fought alongside the British forces in the colonial wars.

During the American Revolution, the desperate efforts of George Washington and the Continental Congress to clothe the soldiers of the patriot army in proper military dress were only partially successful. Many soldiers never received a real uniform at all. It was not until after the Revolution that most of the forces of the United States were properly uniformed. Sailors in the United States Navy were not authorized uniforms until 1841.

This book shows some of the military uniforms—both dress, for formal occasions, and combat, for the battlefield—worn by the American armed forces from 1639 to 1968. These uniforms have varied in cut and color in accordance with the military fashions of the times. For example, at the time of the Civil War, many of the armies of Europe had adopted uniforms cut in the French fashion, so both the Union and Confederate armies fought the war in uniforms patterned, more or less, on those of the army of Napoleon III.

With the advent of the rifled musket, the machine gun, and the high explosive shell, soldiers the world over gradually went into drab, functional, earth-colored combat dress—brilliant uniforms made easy targets on the battlefield. Much of the color and pageantry of the military uniform passed away under the murderous conditions of modern warfare. The uniforms of today retain little to remind us of the gaudy era of scarlet coats, sparkling buttons, and fluttering plumes.

Copyright © 1976 by Dover Publications, Inc. All rights reserved under Pan American and International Copyright Conventions.

Published in Canada by General Publishing Company, Ltd., 30 Lesmill Road, Don Mills, Toronto, Ontario.
Published in the United Kingdom by Constable and Company, Ltd.

American Military Uniforms, 1639-1968, A Coloring Book is a new work, first published by Dover Publications, Inc., in 1976.

DOVER *Pictorial Archive* SERIES

This book belongs to the Dover Pictorial Archive Series. You may use the designs and illustrations for graphics and crafts applications, free and without special permission, provided that you include no more than four in the same publication or project. (For permission for additional use, please write to Dover Publications, Inc., 31 East 2nd Street, Mineola, N.Y. 11501.)
However, republication or reproduction of any illustration by any other graphic service, whether it be in a book or in any other design resource, is strictly prohibited.

International Standard Book Number: 0-486-23239-5

Manufactured in the United States of America. Dover Publications, Inc., 31 East 2nd Street, Mineola, N.Y. 11501.

1. OFFICER OF THE MILITARY COMPANY OF MASSACHUSETTS, 1639. The company was composed of pikemen in half armor and musketeers carrying matchlock muskets. Like the officer shown here, both wore red feathers in their hats and buff coats (worn by the pikemen under their armor). The officer's breeches, breast ribbons, and shoulder knots are scarlet, his stockings white and his boots and hat light brown. His iron-hilted rapier hangs from a light brown belt bordered with gold. His lace collar and cuffs are white. His coat is leather with gold trim.

2. OFFICER OF
NEW YORK MILITIA
TROOP OF HORSE, 1725.

New York raised a number of militia
units early in the 18th century,
among them artillery and cavalry
units and two companies of
cadets. The officer wears a
white wig, a scarlet coat and vest,
both trimmed with silver lace,
buff leather breeches, and black
leather boots with steel spurs.
His neckcloth is white and his waist
belt is of buff leather edged with
silver lace. His sword has a steel
hilt, a silver sword knot, and
a black leather scabbard. His hat
is of black felt edged with
silver lace.

3. OFFICER, SOUTH CAROLINA PROVINCIAL REGIMENT, 1757. The men in Colonel Howarth's Regiment, raised in 1757, were known as "the Buffs," after the color of their facings, and served in what is now Tennessee during one of the Cherokee wars. The officer wears the English-made uniform adopted by the regiment: a dark blue coat cuffed and lined with buff cloth, a buff vest edged with silver lace, and dark blue breeches. His buttonholes are edged with silver lace, as is his black cocked hat. The sash over his shoulder is of crimson silk and his stockings are white. His shoes are of black leather with silver buckles. His wig is white, and his shirt and neckcloth are white linen.

**4. OFFICER,
11TH NEW HAMPSHIRE
PROVINCIAL REGIMENT, 1774.**
Only the officers in this brief-lived
regiment were authorized uniforms.
This one wears a scarlet coat, trimmed
with silver lace. The lapels of
his coat (turned back at the top), his
cuffs, vest, and breeches are sky
blue. His stockings, shirt ruffles, and
neckcloth are white. His hat is of black
felt. His buttons, the lace edging on
his waistcoat, shoulder knot and
crescent-shape gorget are silver. His shoes
are of black leather with silver buckles.

**5. SAILOR, CONNECTICUT
STATE NAVY, 1776.**
States' navies only weakened the efforts of
the Continental Navy in the Revolution.
Instead of a uniform, this gunner
aboard the *Oliver Cromwell* wears
clothing issued to him and the other crew
members of the vessel. He wears
a dark blue jacket with black leather
buttons, a red vest, and blue and
white striped trousers. His neckerchief is
green with white spots. His hat is black
with a white edging on the brim, and his
stockings are striped red and white.
His iron-hilted cutlass hangs from a
black leather belt and rests in a
black leather scabbard. In his left hand
he holds a rammer.

6. COMPANY OFFICER, BUTLER'S RANGERS, 1779.

Basically a unit of frontier raiders, this
Loyalist regiment waged a bloody fight
against the patriot forces. The officer
wears a black cockade, black felt
cocked hat with a gold edging, a
white ruffled shirt, and a dark green
vest and coat with scarlet collar,
lapels, cuffs and lining. His
buttons are brass, and his epaulette
gold. His breeches are of buff
leather. His stockings are gray worsted,
and his short leggings and shoes
are black. Around his waist he wears
a crimson silk sash, and over his
shoulder he wears a yellow, white, red,
and blue Indian beaded belt
with ermine's tails, supporting a
haversack slung behind his left hip. His
sword has a brass hilt and fittings
with white grips and a black
scabbard. His firearm is a frontiersman's
rifle, with steel fittings and a brass
trigger-guard.

**7. INFANTRY OFFICER,
WAYNE'S LEGION, 1794.**
The Legion, which defeated the Indians at
the battle of Fallen Timbers in 1794, was
composed of 4 sub legions, each a miniature
army within itself, with companies of
infantry, riflemen, cavalry, and artillery.
This officer wears the colors of the 2nd Sub
Legion: dark blue breeches and coat with
red collar, cuffs, and lapels, lined with
white; a black hat, and boots. His buttons,
belt plate and spurs are of white metal, as is
his epaulette. His vest is white. His sword
has a brass hilt, and the scabbard is of black
leather. His sword belt is of white leather.

8. ARTILLERY CADET, WEST POINT, 1805.

The first cadets at the Academy were destined for the Artillery and the Corps of Engineers. This cadet wears a uniform which is partly that of a commissioned officer, and partly that of a non-commissioned officer. His coat is dark blue, with red collar, lapels, cuffs and lining. The wings on his coat (at the shoulder below the epaulette) are dark blue with a red edging. His buttons are brass, as is his sword hilt and sword belt plate. His vest and breeches are white, and his boots are black with red edging, and tassel. His hat is of black felt, with a red feather. His sword belt is of white leather and his cartridge pouch, worn at his waist, is of black leather. His musket has steel fittings.

9. ARTILLERY DRUMMER, U.S. ARMY, 1812.

Drummers, fifers, and musicians commonly wore "reverse clothing"; if the regiment wore blue uniforms faced with red, the musicians wore red coats faced with blue. As most musicians of U.S. regiments wore red coats, captured British uniforms were often used to clothe them during the War of 1812. The drummer wears a scarlet coat with brass buttons, and dark blue collar and cuffs. His gaiters (short leggings) are black, as are his shoes and hat (called a *chapeau bras*) with gold tassels, a small gold eagle on the cockade, and a white feather. The braid on his collar is of gold, as is his sword hilt. His breeches are white. His drum has a gold and white eagle on a dark blue field with gold stars. The hoops, at the top and bottom of the drum are red, and the carrying sling and sword belt are of white leather. The braid on his coat front and cuffs is black.

10. SERGEANT, 32ND INFANTRY REGIMENT, U.S. ARMY, 1813.

A member of one of the hastily raised regiments in the War of 1812, he is dressed in a fatigue uniform, and never received a proper dress uniform. His cap is of black leather with a pewter metal plate in front, and a white braided cord and plume at the side. His "roundabout" jacket and his trousers are light blue-gray. His rank is shown by his white epaulette and crimson sash. His canteen is bright red with "U.S." in white. The gaiters he wears beneath his trousers are dark gray, and his shoes are black. The haversack worn beneath his canteen is of white duck, and his knapsack is dark blue. His blanket is green, and his cross belts are of white leather with a white metal or pewter plate. His musket has iron fittings and a white leather strap. His black leather scabbard has a steel tip.

11. FIELD OFFICER,
U.S. MARINE CORPS, 1826.

The green coat worn by the Continental Marines during
the Revolution (and worn by Marines today as part of
the winter field uniform) gave way to the dark
blue worn by the Army and Navy of the nineteenth
century. This officer wears a black hat with gold cord;
a dark blue coat with gold braid and scarlet
cuffs, collar, and lapel; and white trousers and gloves.
His sash is of crimson silk. His sword has a white
ivory hilt; the sword knot, fittings and scabbard are
brass. His waist belt is of white leather with a
brass plate. His epaulettes are gold, his
boots are of black leather.

12. ARTILLERY OFFICER, U.S. ARMY, 1827.
In peacetime this captain wears a black leather cap
with a gold eagle on the front, gold cords and band,
and a yellow pompom. His coat is dark blue.
The wings, shoulder straps, collar braid, buttons,
and the chevrons on his arms are gold.
His waist belt is of white leather with a brass
plate. His trousers are light blue, his gloves are
white, and his sword is in a brass scabbard.
The sash around his waist is of crimson silk. The
braid on the front of his coat is black.

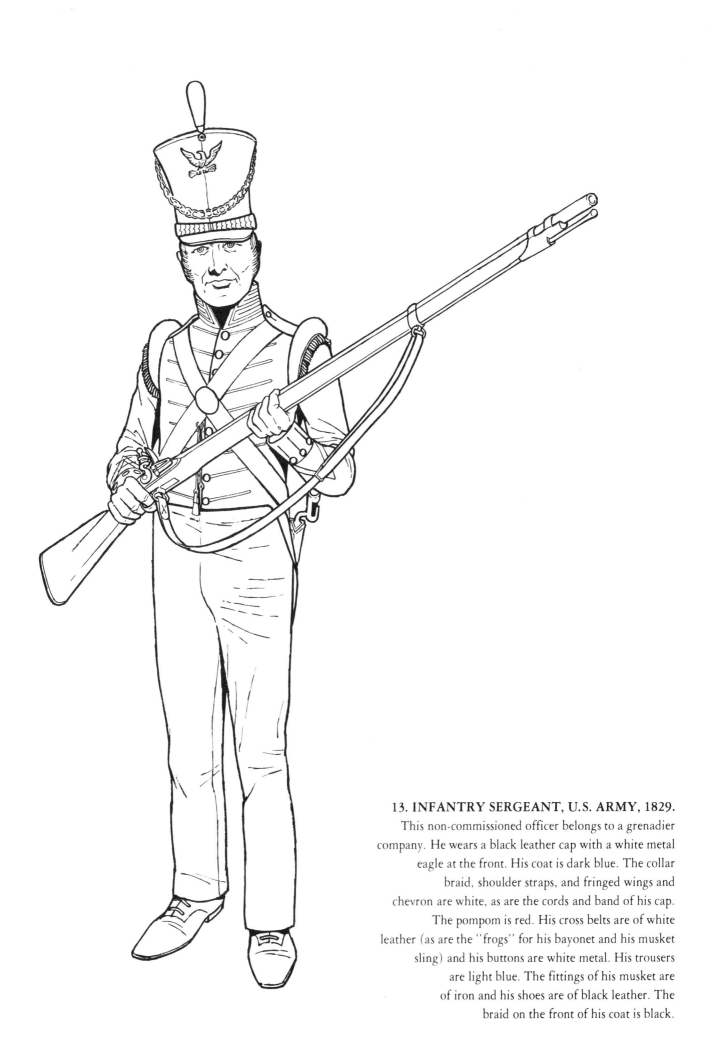

13. INFANTRY SERGEANT, U.S. ARMY, 1829.
This non-commissioned officer belongs to a grenadier
company. He wears a black leather cap with a white metal
eagle at the front. His coat is dark blue. The collar
braid, shoulder straps, and fringed wings and
chevron are white, as are the cords and band of his cap.
The pompom is red. His cross belts are of white
leather (as are the "frogs" for his bayonet and his musket
sling) and his buttons are white metal. His trousers
are light blue. The fittings of his musket are
of iron and his shoes are of black leather. The
braid on the front of his coat is black.

14. MEDICAL OFFICER, U.S. NAVY, 1830.
This assistant surgeon is in the undress uniform of
1830–1841. While the dress uniforms of the military
services of this time were elaborate, the
undress uniform often tended to approximate the
civilian dress of the day. He wears a black hat, with
black cockade and gold cord, and a dark blue
coat with brass buttons. His waist belt and sword
slings are of white leather and his trousers are white.
His shoes are of black leather, as is his sword
scabbard with brass fittings. His sword has
white grips, brass hilt, and gold sword knot.

15. BOATSWAIN, U.S. REVENUE CUTTER SERVICE, 1834.

The U.S. Revenue Cutter Service became the U.S. Coast Guard in 1915. This is uniform dress prescribed for seamen and petty officers. The jacket is dark blue with brass buttons. The neckerchief, shoes, hat, and ribbon are black. The shirt, or frock, is white with a light blue front enclosed within the stripes. The trousers are white. The boatswain wears a silver whistle around his neck as a symbol of his rank. The collar of his shirt is light blue with white stripes and stars.

16. SERGEANT, BRISBANE'S REGIMENT, SOUTH CAROLINA MILITIA, 1836.

Members of this regiment, raised for the Seminole
War, wore different uniforms; some had none
at all. The sergeant wears a brown civilian felt
hat with a red, white, and blue cockade.
His green-fringed hunting shirt and trousers
are of brown homespun. His under shirt is
of a pale yellow unbleached linen. His belts and
scabbard are of black leather, and his sash,
worn under his waist belt, is red. His canteen
is light blue with white initials, and
his sword has a brass hilt. His leggings are
of light brown and his shoes are black. His
powder horn, slung at his right side by
a leather thong, is light yellow-brown. He wears
a small rifleman's knife in a sheath on
the shoulder belt which supports his shot
pouch behind his right hip. His long rifle has a
steel lock and brass trigger guard and
patch box on the lower end of the butt. The
outfit resembles a woodsman's.

17. ORDNANCE SERGEANT,
U.S. ARMY, 1836.

This non-commissioned officer took care of
weapons, ammunition, and stores at
military posts. He wears a dark blue coat with
brass buttons, and yellow braid on the
collar, cuffs, and epaulettes. His cap is of
black leather, with a brass eagle and
crossed cannons on the front, and a red plume.
His sword belt is of white leather with a
brass plate. His sash is red, and his trousers are
of light blue with a dark blue stripe down
the side. His sword, in a black leather scabbard,
has a black leather hilt and iron metal fittings.

18. CORPORAL, 3RD INFANTRY REGIMENT, U.S. ARMY, 1846.
This NCO (non-commissioned officer) wears the winter field uniform worn by the infantry during the war with Mexico. His cap is of dark blue cloth with black leather strap and visor. His jacket and trousers are of light blue, the collar of the jacket is worked with white braid, which also edges the shoulder straps. His corporal's stripes are white, as are his waist belt, shoulder belt, and haversack (worn under his canteen, which is red with white lettering). His waist belt has a brass plate. His knapsack is black, and his blanket, rolled on top, is red. His buttons are of white metal. His musket has steel fittings and a wooden stock.

19. SERGEANT, FIRST DRAGOON REGIMENT, U.S. ARMY, 1849.

The regiment was first raised in 1833 to fight the Indians and protect the caravans of covered wagons. On frontier service the troopers wore a simpler uniform than the dress uniform shown here. The sergeant wears a leather cap on the front of which is a silver eagle in a brass sunburst. Its cords are yellow; the plumes are white. His coat is dark blue with yellow collar, chevrons, and cuffs trimmed with gold braid, which also edges the tails of his coat. His belts are of white leather. His black leather cartridge box, worn in the middle of his back, has a brass plate. His trousers are light blue with yellow stripes up the sides. His sword is in a steel scabbard, and his carbine, slung from the shoulder by a white leather belt, is of iron with a wooden stock. His shoes are of black leather; his spurs are of brass, as are the metal scales on his shoulders and his buckles. His gloves are white.

20. MIDSHIPMAN, U.S. NAVY, 1852.
This undress uniform was established by a regulation
of 1852, and was worn throughout the Civil War. His
cap is dark blue with a gold band about the
bottom of the crown; the visor and chin strap are
of black leather. The device on the front
of the cap is a silver anchor in a gold wreath.
His coat and trousers are dark blue with
brass buttons. His shoulder strap and trouser stripes
are gold. His shoes and belt are of black leather,
and his belt buckle is brass. His sword has
a white leather grip and brass fittings. The scabbard
is of black leather with brass fittings, and
his sword knot is of gold.

21. FIRST SERGEANT, LIGHT ARTILLERY, U.S. ARMY, 1855.

The jacket is dark blue, with red piping on the edges, cuffs and collar, the color of the artillery. His sergeant's stripes and his sash are also red, as is the peaked welt of cloth around the crown of his cap and the pompom. The cap has a dark blue top, black leather visor and a brass insignia on the front. His trousers are sky blue, and his shoes, waist belt, and sword knot are of black leather. The belt buckle is of brass, as is the hilt of his sword, which has a steel scabbard.

22. PRIVATE, 83RD PENNSYLVANIA VOLUNTEER INFANTRY REGIMENT, U.S. ARMY, 1861.

The regiment is reported to have fought in more battles and lost more men in the Civil War than any other Pennsylvania regiment. This uniform was modeled on that of the French Chasseurs. The cap and coat are dark blue, both edged in yellow braid, with white metal buttons and gold epaulettes. His shoes and belts are of black leather. The trousers are light blue-gray, and the gaiters have light brown tops and are white at the lower parts around the ankles. The overcoat, rolled atop the knapsack behind the soldier's shoulders, is medium gray. The musket has steel fittings, its sling is of brown leather.

23. PRIVATE, 4TH TEXAS VOLUNTEER INFANTRY REGIMENT, C.S. ARMY, 1861.
The private is in the uniform worn by the regiment when the famed Hood's Texas Brigade first arrived in Virginia in 1861. He wears a black felt hat with a silver star. His uniform coat and trousers are of Confederate gray, with black trim. His canteen has a light brown cloth cover, and his belts and cartridge box are of black leather. The cartridge box has a brass plate upon it with a Texas star. His blanket roll is green. His Bowie knife has a wooden handle and a brown leather sheath. His shoes are of brown leather. His Enfield musket, with a sling of white duck cloth, has iron fittings.

24. VIVANDIERE, 114TH PENNSYLVANIA VOLUNTEER INFANTRY REGIMENT ("COLLIS ZOUAVES"), U.S. ARMY, 1862.

A number of regiments raised at the beginning of the Civil War were patterned on the French colonial Zouave Regiments from North Africa. The vivandière traveled with the regiment, tending the soldiers in battle, and serving drinks from her small keg. She wears a straw hat with a black ribbon and ostrich plume. Her jacket and skirt, both trimmed in scarlet, are dark blue. Her buttons are brass, as are the metal fittings on the keg. Her blouse is white, and her sash is crimson. Her waist belt and pistol holster are of black leather, as are her shoes. Her trousers are scarlet. Both the vivandieres and the colorful (but impractical) Zouave uniforms disappeared after the first months of the war.

25. MAJOR, VIRGINIA CAVALRY, C.S. ARMY, 1863.
Jeb Stuart and the officers of his famous cavalry unit wore their own distinctive variation of regulation uniform. This officer wears a broad-brimmed, black-plumed, gray felt hat caught up on one side with a silver star. His short cavalry jacket (with yellow lining), the lapels turned back at the top, is Confederate gray, as is his vest. His collar is yellow, the cavalry color, and his Major's star is embroidered in gold. He wears a red checked shirt and a yellow silk sash. His buttons and belt clasp are of brass, and the braid on the sleeves of his jacket is gold. His gauntlets are pale buff leather. His trousers are a light brown corduroy. His boots are of black leather as are his belt and pistol holster, the tip of which can be seen beneath his right arm. His sword has a black leather grip, brass metal fittings and a steel scabbard, and his spurs are brass.

26. CORPORAL OF HEAVY ARTILLERY, CORPS D'AFRIQUE, U.S. ARMY, 1863.

The Corps d'Afrique, composed of black soldiers, was
raised in 1862. Its heavy artillery unit defended
New Orleans after its capture by Federal forces.
This soldier wears a dark blue coat edged
and trimmed with red. His hat is black with a brass
insignia at the side. His waist belt, the
scabbard of his short artillery sword, and his
shoes are of black leather. His buttons, belt plate,
shoulder scales, and the hilt and fittings of
his sword are of brass. His trousers are sky blue
with red stripes down the sides. His corporal's
stripes are red. His musket sling is of
brown leather. His gloves are white.

27. PRIVATE FIRST CLASS, 7TH CAVALRY REGIMENT, U.S. ARMY, 1876.

This is the field uniform of the troopers of the 7th cavalry, five troops of which perished with General George A. Custer at the battle of the Little Big Horn in 1876. This soldier wears a dark gray slouch hat with yellow cord. His kerchief is either red or yellow, and his jacket is dark blue. His private's stripe is yellow, and his cartridge belt, with a brass buckle, is of black leather as are his pistol holster, carbine sling, slings on his saber, and boots. His gloves are pale buff, and his trousers are sky blue. His saber (none were worn at Little Big Horn) has brass fittings and a steel scabbard. His carbine has iron fittings and his spurs are of brass.

28. PRIVATE,
71ST NEW YORK REGIMENT, 1898.

The 71st fought in Cuba during the Spanish-
American war. The soldier wears a light brown felt
hat and leggings, a dark blue jacket with brass
buttons, and light blue pack, canteen with dark blue
initials, and trousers with dark blue stripes. His
shoes are dark brown. His shelter tent,
half rolled above the knapsack, is dark gray. His
valise, slung below the canteen, is black.
His haversack, at the bottom of his pack, is light
blue with dark blue initials. His bayonet scabbard,
projecting from beneath the valise, is
steel. His drinking cup is of unpainted tin. He
carries a Krag Jorgensen magazine rifle, though
most of the militia carried the old
single-shot Springfield.

**29. CORPORAL, 1ST VOLUNTEER
CAVALRY, U.S. ARMY, 1898.**
The "Rough Riders," led by Col. Leonard Wood
and Theodore Roosevelt, became famous for their
charge up San Juan Hill in the Spanish-American
War. This non-commissioned officer wears
stable dress—a light brown slouch hat with brass
cavalry insignia, a khaki jacket and trousers, and
a brown leather pistol belt, holster and shoulder
strap. His corporal's stripes are in cavalry yellow.
His boots are of black leather with steel spurs.
His undershirt is red, and his gauntlets
are of pale buff.

**30. CAPTAIN OF INFANTRY,
U.S. ARMY, 1907.**
This full-dress uniform consists of a cap with a dark
blue top, a light Infantry blue band around the crown
(which is edged with gold) and a gold chin strap
and insignia at the front. The coat is dark blue,
with a light blue collar edged with gold,
brass buttons, and gold sleeve insignia and shoulder
straps. The belt is of gold with a brass buckle;
the sword (with black grip) and scabbard are
steel. His trousers are sky blue with a white stripe
and his boots are of polished black
leather with steel spurs.

31. MACHINIST'S MATE SECOND CLASS, U.S. NAVY, 1908.

This uniform was worn by enlisted men of the Navy
from the late 19th century through World War I.
The blue uniform was the winter uniform; the
summer uniform, of similar cut, was white. The sailor
wears a flat-top cap with the name of his vessel
embroidered on a black silk band around the crown.
His jumper, worn tucked into his trousers, is
dark blue, the collar and cuffs having three white
stripes bordering them, as did the uniforms
worn by Petty Officers and Seamen First Class. His
trousers are dark blue with black buttons.
His shoes are of black leather, and the rating
badge on his sleeve shows a white eagle
and stripes, and a red propeller.

**32. ENSIGN,
U.S. NAVY AVIATION SERVICE, 1917.**
The aviator seen here is wearing an unofficial
uniform adopted in 1914, a combination of Navy
and Marine Corps dress. The cap has a khaki
top, a gold chin strap, and silver Navy insignia in
front. The coat is khaki, with brass buttons. The
pilot's wings over the left pocket are gold, as
are the shoulder star and stripe. The khaki
breeches and brown wraparound leggings are
Marine Corps issue. His shoes are black leather
Navy issue. The uniform became the official summer
uniform of flying officers of the Navy in 1917.

33. CAPTAIN OF ARTILLERY, AMERICAN EXPEDITIONARY FORCE, U.S. ARMY, 1918.

This field service uniform was adopted in the first years of the 20th century, and was worn by the Army and Marine Corps in France during World War I. The captain wears a steel helmet painted drab brown or green. His jacket and breeches are olive drab, with buttons and collar insignia of dull bronze. His rank is indicated by the silver bars on his shoulder straps and the brown strip of braid on his sleeve. His waist belt, boots and pistol holster are of brown leather, while his pistol belt and the wide belt over his right shoulder are tan web.

**34. LIEUTENANT,
U.S. ARMY SIGNAL CORPS
(AVIATION SERVICE), 1918.**
The pilot is wearing one style of dress worn in
the air in combat over France in World War I.
His flying helmet and Sam Brown belt are
of brown leather and his flying coat is tan,
with a brown fur collar. His uniform tunic,
worn beneath the flying coat, is of olive drab,
as are his breeches. His buttons are a
dull bronze. His flying boots are dark brown.
He leans against a fighter plane that
would be camouflaged green and brown.

35. LIEUTENANT, U.S. ARMY TANK CORPS, ARMORED FORCES, 1938.

This officer in field uniform is wearing a brown reinforced leather crash helmet with fleece-lined goggles. His shirt, breeches, and web waist belt are khaki. His web pistol belt is brown. His map case, worn on his left side, is brown canvas. His binocular case, slung behind his right arm, is of brown leather, as are the straps crossing over his chest, his boots, and his pistol holster. The collar insignia are of brass.

36. PRIVATE, INFANTRY, U.S. ARMY, 1943.

This infantryman wears a uniform typical of the European Theater of Operations of World War II. His steel helmet, painted olive drab, is covered with a camouflage netting. His field jacket is khaki; his cartridge belt is brown. His haversack, slung at his side, and his knapsack and leggings, worn over brown shoes, are tan. His bayonet has a black handle and a gray scabbard. His trousers are olive drab. His private's chevron is light brown with a dark brown border.

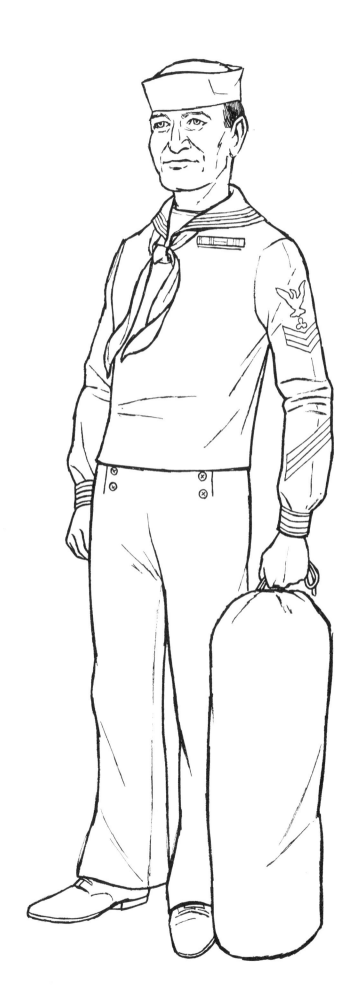

37. MACHINIST'S MATE FIRST CLASS, U.S. NAVY, 1945.

This Petty Officer is wearing "dress blues," the winter dress uniform of the Naval enlisted man. His cap is white, and his jumper and trousers (with black buttons) are dark blue. His collar and cuffs are bordered with three white stripes. His shoes are of black leather, and his sea bag is white. On his left arm he wears his Petty Officer's rating badge. The eagle is white and stripes, or inverted chevrons, and the machinist's propeller are red. Below this he wears three red "hash marks" signifying three enlistments in the Navy. His neckerchief is black, and his campaign ribbons, worn above his breast pocket, are of various bright colors.

38. SERGEANT, U.S. MARINE CORPS, 1945.
This is the winter service uniform. The cap, coat, and
trousers are of forest green, with black buttons and lapel
insignia. His leather waist belt is black, as are his
shoes. The sergeant's stripes are yellow, edged in
red, as are his "hash marks." His shirt is tan, as is his
tie. His campaign, or service, ribbons, worn above
his left breast pocket, are of various bright colors.

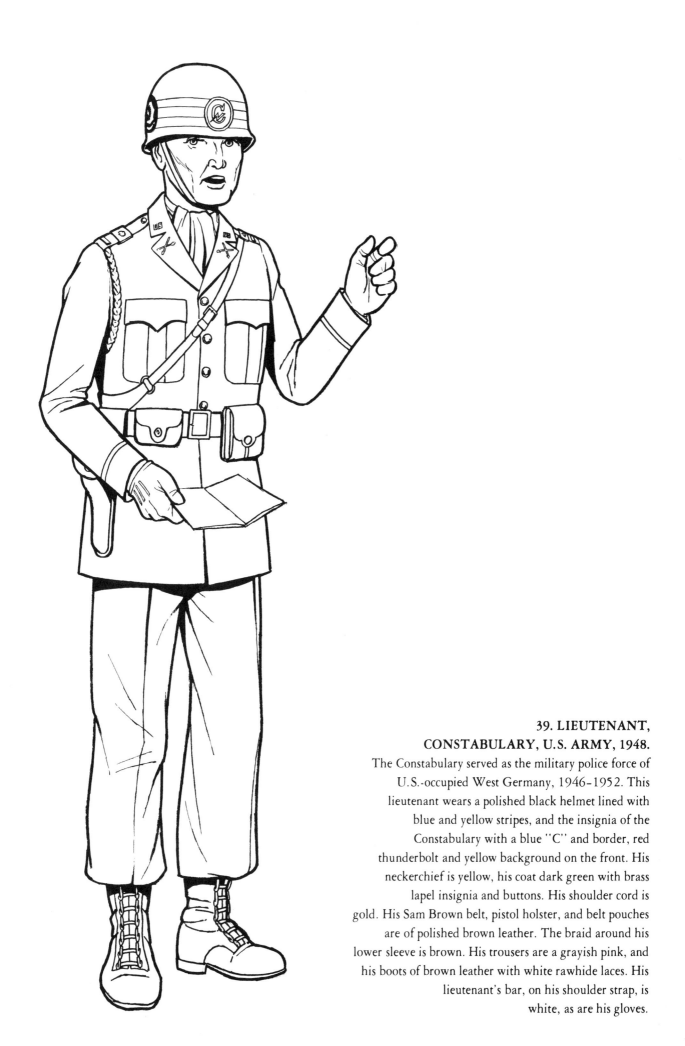

**39. LIEUTENANT,
CONSTABULARY, U.S. ARMY, 1948.**
The Constabulary served as the military police force of
U.S.-occupied West Germany, 1946–1952. This
lieutenant wears a polished black helmet lined with
blue and yellow stripes, and the insignia of the
Constabulary with a blue "C" and border, red
thunderbolt and yellow background on the front. His
neckerchief is yellow, his coat dark green with brass
lapel insignia and buttons. His shoulder cord is
gold. His Sam Brown belt, pistol holster, and belt pouches
are of polished brown leather. The braid around his
lower sleeve is brown. His trousers are a grayish pink, and
his boots of brown leather with white rawhide laces. His
lieutenant's bar, on his shoulder strap, is
white, as are his gloves.

**40. PRIVATE, FIRST CAVALRY DIVISION,
U.S. ARMY, 1950.**
This soldier is in field dress worn in Korea. His cap is
of brown fur, and his neckerchief is cavalry yellow.
His field jacket and trousers are olive drab. His
cartridge belt and suspender belts are tan. His gloves
are yellow leather. His boots are of brown
leather. In his hand he holds a Browning automatic
rifle with all steel metal fittings.

41. DRUM MAJOR, U.S. ARMY, 1954.

Bandsmen have always been the most colorfully
dressed soldiers in the army. This one is in winter full
dress uniform. His cap has a dark blue top and a
yellow band around the crown. The chin strap
and visor are of black leather. His coat is yellow,
with dark blue collar, cuffs, and braid trimmings. His
collar, cap insignia, buttons, and belt plate
are of brass. His belt is of white leather.
His trousers are dark blue with a yellow stripe. His
shoes are of black leather and his staff is of
natural wood color with a silver knob at
the top, and white cords around it. His shoulder
straps are dark blue.

**42. LIEUTENANT,
U.S. MARINE CORPS, 1954.**
This company-grade officer is wearing the blue
undress uniform with a boat cloak over it. His
cap is dark blue. The chin strap and Marine
Corps device are gold. His coat is navy blue
with gold buttons, insignia and belt buckle.
His trousers, with a scarlet stripe,
are also blue, somewhat darker than sky blue,
but not as dark as the blue of the coat.
His shoes and visor are of black leather. His
boat cloak is of dark blue, with a scarlet
lining, a black velvet collar, and a black
cord fastening at the top.

43. CORPORAL, WOMEN'S ARMY CORPS, 1955.
The Corps was raised in 1942. Its uniform in the 1950s
was the same as that of the Army Nurse Corps, but with
different insignia. This corporal wears the summer
service uniform. Her cap, dress, and belt are tan. Her
buttons and collar and cap insignia are brass,
and the chevrons on her sleeve are yellow. Over her
shoulder she carries a white handbag with brass
clasp. Her stockings are flesh colored, and
her shoes are light brown.

44. CAPTAIN, U.S. AIR FORCE, 1961.
The Air Force has tried to keep the uniform plain, yet
distinctive. This officer is wearing the winter service
uniform, which is of a color described by the Air
Force as "Blue, Shade 84"—a medium blue,
with a touch of gray in it. His cap, coat, trousers,
and tie are of this color. The visor of his cap,
the chinstrap, and his shoes are of black leather.
The captain's bars on his shoulder straps are
of silver, as are his Air Force wings, worn over his
service ribbons above the left breast pocket.
His cap device buttons and lapel insignia are
white metal. His shirt is sky blue.

45. PRIVATE, 101ST AIRBORNE DIVISION, U.S. ARMY, 1968.

The paratrooper wears the typical field service uniform worn by airborne and infantry units in Vietnam. His soft hat is camouflaged in patches of green and brown. His jacket, trousers and backpack are olive drab, which soon faded under the tropical sun and monsoon rains to a pale gray-green. His canteen covers are buff-colored web material. The groundsheet and air mattress enclosed within his backpack are a medium gray. His M-16 rifle is black, and his jungle boots are light brown with dark brown heels and toes. On his right sleeve he wears the shoulder patch of the division—a white eagle's head with yellow beak within a black shield. His machete has a steel blade and a black handle.